BEST OF
EGG

GARDEN *of* GRAPES.

First Edition: 2023

Published by Garden of Grapes.

Printed in USA

Library of Congress Cataloging-in-Publication Data:

First edition.
Includes index.

Manufactured in USA

Introduction

Ladies and gentlemen, culinary comrades, and fellow egg enthusiasts, welcome to the world of sizzling pans, delicate flips, and the extraordinary universe that is the "Best of Eggs Cookbook: Crack & Cook."

As we embark on this egg-centric journey, allow me to extend a heartfelt welcome, a virtual handshake, and a seat at the breakfast table. This cookbook is not just a collection of recipes; it's a celebration of the incredible versatility and humble magnificence of the egg.

So, why eggs, you might ask? Well, my friends, the inspiration behind this culinary escapade is simple yet profound. The egg, in its unassuming shell, holds unparalleled potential. It's the canvas upon which we paint breakfasts, brunches, lunches, and dinners —a versatile medium that transcends boundaries and cultures.

Picture this: a crack, a sizzle, and the aroma that fills the kitchen, awakening your senses to the endless possibilities that lie within that simple shell. That, my friends, is the magic of eggs, and this cookbook is a tribute to their culinary prowess.

In these pages, you'll find a curated selection of over 100 delectable creations, each crafted to showcase the egg's ability to transform into culinary masterpieces. From the classic sunny-side-up to the more adventurous soufflés and frittatas, we're diving deep into the world of egg-centric delights.

But it's not just about recipes. This cookbook is a journey—a gastronomic expedition where each page is a step into the realm of crackling shells, velvety yolks, and fluffy whites. Expect a symphony of flavors, textures, and techniques that will empower you to master the art of egg cookery, whether you're a seasoned chef or a kitchen novice.

In these recipes, you'll discover the stories of cultures, the comfort of home-cooked meals, and the sheer joy of creating something extraordinary from the simplest of ingredients. So, fasten your aprons, sharpen your knives, and get ready to embark on a culinary adventure that celebrates the egg in all its crackling glory.

With immense pleasure and an egg in hand, let's crack, cook, and revel in the extraordinary world of eggs. Welcome to the "Best of Eggs Cookbook: Crack & Cook." May your culinary journey be as egg-citing and egg-straordinary as the recipes within these pages!

Cooking Philosophy or Approach

In the realm of eggs, where the simplicity of a shell conceals culinary magic, this cookbook is more than just a collection of recipes; it's a manifesto, a celebration of the humble yet extraordinary egg. So, what's the philosophy that simmers beneath the surface?

Firstly, it's about embracing the egg as a culinary canvas. From the delicate poached perfection to the hearty embrace of a well-constructed omelet, each dish is a stroke of artistry. The egg, in its various forms, becomes a palette for flavors, textures, and the unbridled joy of cracking into something extraordinary.

Secondly, it's a nod to the timeless nature of eggs. Whether you're a novice cook or a seasoned chef, the egg is your ally. It's versatile, forgiving, and open to interpretation. This cookbook encourages experimentation—swap ingredients, tweak techniques, make it your own. Eggs, after all, are the ultimate collaborators in the kitchen.

Now, let's talk technique. The recipes within these pages aren't just about cooking eggs; they're about mastering them. Whether you're perfecting the art of the flip for a flawless sunny-side-up or delicately whisking up a soufflé, the techniques outlined are meant to elevate your egg game. This is not just a cookbook; it's your guide to becoming an egg maestro.

As for ingredients, simplicity is key. The focus is on the quality of the eggs themselves. Farm-fresh, free-range, organic—the cookbook encourages you to source the best eggs you can find. Because, in the world of eggs, the quality of the main ingredient can make or break the dish.

Styles? Think of this cookbook as a world tour of egg-centric delights. From classic French techniques to adventurous fusion twists, it covers a spectrum as broad as the versatility of the egg itself. It's an invitation to explore, discover, and savor the myriad ways eggs can dance on your taste buds.

In essence, this cookbook is a tribute to the egg, a humble yet extraordinary culinary cornerstone. It's an exploration of flavors, an ode to technique, and a celebration of the extraordinary potential packed within that unassuming shell. So, crack on, fellow cooks, and let the egg adventures begin!

Tips for Successful Cooking

Welcome to the sacred realm of egg mastery, where the seemingly simple act of cracking becomes a culinary rite. In this section, I won't sermonize; I'll share practical insights to elevate your egg game. So, grab your apron, and let's dive into the alchemy of eggs.

1. The Sacred Crack:
   - Crack eggs on a flat surface, not the edge of a bowl. It minimizes shell fragments and ensures a clean break. A perfect crack sets the tone for a perfect dish.

2. The Fresher, the Better:
   - Fresh eggs make a world of difference. The whites hold their shape, and the yolks stand tall. Invest in quality, and let your eggs rise to the occasion.

3. Temperature Matters:
   - Bring eggs to room temperature before cooking. Cold eggs can lead to uneven cooking, affecting the texture of your dish. Let your eggs bask in the warmth of the kitchen.

4. The Art of Whisking:
   - When whisking, use a gentle hand. Vigorous whisking introduces air, giving a light and airy texture to your creations. Save the muscle for the gym; here, finesse is key.

5. The Low and Slow Rule:
   - Whether scrambling or making custards, cook eggs over low heat. Patience pays off, and your eggs will reward you with a silky, velvety texture.

6. The Versatile Seasoning:

- Seasoning is an art. Salt enhances, pepper elevates, and herbs dance on the palate. Experiment, but remember, a pinch can be mightier than a pound.

7. The Perfect Flip:

- If you're flipping an omelet or a frittata, do it with confidence. Use a spatula, not hope. The perfect flip is an assertion of culinary prowess.

8. The Poaching Ballet:

- Poaching eggs is like a delicate ballet. Use fresh eggs, create a gentle vortex in simmering water, and slide the eggs in. It's poetry in motion.

9. The Resting Ritual:

- Let your eggs rest. Whether it's allowing hard-boiled eggs to cool or letting a frittata set, patience allows flavors to harmonize.

10. Trust Your Instincts:

- Cooking eggs is an intuitive dance. Trust your instincts. The sizzle, the aroma—let them guide you to egg perfection.

These tips are your compass, not your shackles. So, go forth, dear reader, and let the crack of the egg be your overture to a symphony of delectable creations. May your yolks be runny, your whites be fluffy, and your egg journey be nothing short of egg-cellent!

Kitchen Essentials

Welcome to the kitchen, the battleground where a cook armed with the right tools conquers the mighty egg. In this section, we're not just talking about spatulas and pans; we're delving into the arsenal that transforms your kitchen into an egg-cooking sanctuary.

1. The Noble Whisk:
   - A true knight in shining armor, the whisk is your weapon for achieving the perfect scramble and fluffiest omelet. Embrace it, wield it with finesse, and watch your eggs transform.

2. The Non-Stick Pan:
   - The non-stick pan is your trusty steed, gliding through the realm of eggs without a hitch. From delicate crepes to crispy fried eggs, this is the backbone of your egg-cooking kingdom.

3. The Egg Timer:
   - Time is of the essence in the egg world. An egg timer ensures your soft-boiled eggs are just the right amount of gooey. Say goodbye to overcooked disappointment.

4. The Silicone Spatula:
   - Your versatile sidekick in the egg battle. It's nimble enough to flip a delicate omelet and sturdy enough to tackle a hearty scramble. The silicone spatula is your go-to tool for egg mastery.

5. The Egg Poacher:
   - A mystical device that turns the challenging art of poaching into a breeze. The egg poacher ensures perfectly poached eggs, with runny yolks that are nothing short of divine.

6. The Grater:
   - Not just for cheese, a grater becomes your secret weapon for adding a flurry of flavors to your egg dishes. Grate some cheese, herbs, or veggies to elevate your creations.

7. The Mandoline Slicer:

- Transform ordinary ingredients into stunning garnishes with the mandoline slicer. Picture thinly sliced veggies enhancing the visual appeal of your frittatas and egg bakes.

8. The Immersion Blender:

- A wizard's wand in the kitchen. The immersion blender helps you whip up dreamy, airy eggs for soufflés and meringues. It's the magic touch your egg desserts deserve.

Tips on Wielding Your Arsenal:

- Temperature Mastery:

Master the flame. Different egg dishes require different heat levels. Scrambles like it hot, while delicate omelets prefer a gentle dance with the flame.

- Preparation Prowess:

Prep before you conquer. Crack your eggs into a separate bowl, ensuring no rogue shells invade your culinary kingdom.

- Seasoning Savvy:

Salt is your ally, but wield it wisely. Season eggs just before cooking to avoid moisture loss, ensuring a velvety texture.

- Freshness is Key:

The fresher the eggs, the better the dish. Invest in quality eggs to truly unleash the potential of your egg creations.

Equip yourself with these tools and tips, and you'll wield the spatula like a culinary knight, conquering eggs with unparalleled finesse. May your kitchen reign be filled with cracking successes and eggcellent triumphs!

Flavor Pairing Suggestions

Welcome to the flavor playground, where eggs transform into masterpieces. Here are some suggestions to inspire your culinary escapades and encourage you to create your own egg symphony:

1. The Classic Harmony:
   - Start with the timeless duo of eggs and butter. Whether scrambled, poached, or fried, the rich, creamy notes of butter enhance the natural goodness of eggs.

2. Herbaceous Ballet:
   - Elevate your eggs with the vibrant dance of herbs. Think chives with scrambled eggs, dill on a poached egg, or basil in an omelet. Herbs add layers of freshness and fragrance.

3. Umami Unison:
   - Enter the world of umami by pairing eggs with ingredients like mushrooms, soy sauce, or miso. The savory richness of umami complements the inherent creaminess of eggs.

4. Cheesy Serenade:
   - Cheese and eggs—a match made in culinary heaven. Whether it's a sprinkle of Parmesan on your frittata or the gooey goodness of melted cheddar on scrambled eggs, cheese adds a comforting melody.

5. Veggie Waltz:
   - Let your eggs dance with a medley of vegetables. Spinach, tomatoes, bell peppers—the crisp textures and vibrant colors create a harmonious balance.

6. Smoked Symphony:
   - Introduce smoky flavors with ingredients like bacon or smoked salmon. The smokiness adds depth and complexity, turning your eggs into a savory masterpiece.

7. Spicy Fusion:

- Kick up the heat with a dash of hot sauce, a sprinkle of chili flakes, or the subtle warmth of paprika. Spice adds a lively note to your egg creations.

8. Citrus Elegance:

- Brighten up your eggs with a squeeze of citrus. Lemon or lime zest can add a zingy freshness, especially to dishes like eggs benedict or a citrus-infused omelet.

9. Breakfast Symphony:

- Merge eggs with breakfast classics like avocado, sausage, or hash browns. The combination creates a hearty, soul-warming melody perfect for a morning feast.

10. Global Fusion:

- Take a trip around the world by incorporating flavors from different cuisines. Try curry-spiced eggs, or pair them with salsa for a Mexican twist.

Remember, these are merely notes in your culinary sheet music. Feel free to experiment, improvise, and let your taste buds be the conductor. The Best of Eggs Cookbook is your kitchen's stage—may your creations be as extraordinary as the potential within each cracked shell. Happy cooking!

Table of contents

Chapter 1:
Classic Egg Breakfasts

2 servings   220 cal   10 min

Perfect Scrambled Eggs

The epitome of morning comfort, these creamy eggs will melt your heart.

Ingredients:

- 4 large eggs
- 2 tbsp butter
- Salt and pepper, to taste

Directions

1. Crack the eggs into a bowl. Beat them until well combined.
2. Heat a non-stick pan over low heat and melt the butter.
3. Pour in the beaten eggs and stir continuously until creamy.
4. Season with salt and pepper to taste. Serve hot.

Fun Facts

Did you know? Scrambled eggs were a favorite of Ernest Hemingway.

1 omelette 320 cal 15 min

Fluffy Omelette with Cheese

This cheesy omelette is like a warm, savory hug on your plate.

Ingredients:

- 3 large eggs
- 1/4 cup shredded cheddar cheese
- Salt and pepper, to taste

Directions

1. Crack the eggs into a bowl and beat them.
2. Heat a non-stick pan over medium heat.
3. Pour the beaten eggs into the pan and cook until set.
4. Sprinkle cheese on one half and fold the other half over.
5. Cook for another minute until cheese melts. Serve hot.

Fun Facts

Omelettes originated in France and were named after the word "amelette," which means a thin sheet or layer.

2 servings   450 cal   25 min

A classic brunch favorite with poached eggs, crispy bacon, and rich hollandaise sauce.

Eggs Benedict with Hollandaise

Ingredients:

- 4 large eggs
- 2 English muffins
- 4 slices of Canadian bacon
- Hollandaise sauce
- Chopped chives for garnish

Directions

1. Toast the English muffins and cook the Canadian bacon.
2. Poach the eggs to your desired doneness.
3. Place a slice of bacon on each muffin half.
4. Top with a poached egg and hollandaise sauce.
5. Garnish with chopped chives. Serve hot.

Fun Facts

Eggs Benedict was invented in the late 19th century by a New York stockbroker who wanted a cure for his hangover.

2 servings   350 cal   15 min

Classic Eggs and Bacon

The timeless pairing of crispy bacon and perfectly fried eggs.

Ingredients:

- 4 large eggs
- 8 strips of bacon
- Salt and pepper, to taste

Directions

1. Heat a pan over medium heat and cook the bacon until crispy.
2. Remove bacon and drain on paper towels.
3. In the same pan, fry the eggs sunny side up.
4. Season with salt and pepper. Serve with bacon.

Fun Facts

The term "bacon" is derived from the Old High German word "bacho," meaning the back of the pig.

2 servings 250 cal 20 min

Poached Eggs on Toast

A simple yet elegant dish, where perfectly poached eggs sit atop golden toast.

Ingredients:

- 4 large eggs
- 2 slices of toasted bread
- Butter for spreading
- Vinegar
- Salt and pepper, to taste

Directions

1. Toast the bread and spread with butter.
2. Fill a pan with water, add vinegar, and bring to a simmer.
3. Crack eggs into separate cups and gently slide them into the simmering water.
4. Poach for 3-4 minutes.
5. Place poached eggs on the toast, season, and serve.

Fun Facts

The first known recipe for poached eggs appeared in a Roman cookbook from the 4th century.

2 servings 380 cal 20 min

Spanish Chorizo and Eggs

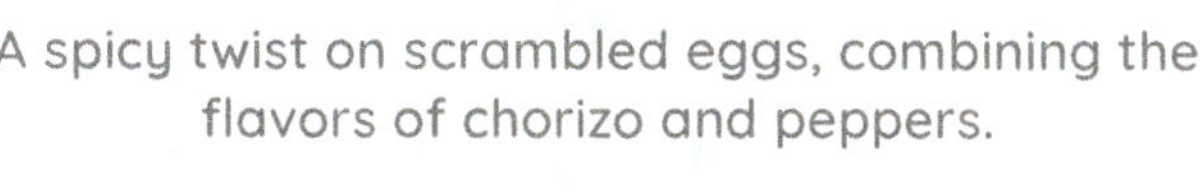

A spicy twist on scrambled eggs, combining the flavors of chorizo and peppers.

Ingredients:

- 4 large eggs
- 1/2 cup diced Spanish chorizo
- 1/2 cup diced bell peppers
- 2 tbsp olive oil
- Salt and pepper, to taste

Directions

1. Heat olive oil in a pan over medium heat.
2. Add chorizo and peppers, sauté until chorizo is browned and peppers are tender.
3. Beat eggs and pour over the mixture.
4. Scramble until cooked.
5. Season with salt and pepper. Serve hot.

Fun Facts

Chorizo is a type of sausage that originated in the Iberian Peninsula and is used in many Spanish and Mexican dishes.

2 servings   320 cal   25 min

A Mexican breakfast classic featuring fried eggs, salsa, and tortillas.

Huevos Rancheros

Ingredients:

- 4 large eggs
- 4 small corn tortillas
- 1 cup salsa
- 1/2 cup refried beans
- Chopped cilantro and crumbled queso fresco for garnish

Directions

1. Heat the tortillas and keep warm.
2. Fry the eggs sunny side up.
3. Warm the refried beans.
4. Place a tortilla on each plate and spread beans on top.
5. Top with fried eggs, salsa, cilantro, and queso fresco.

Fun Facts

Huevos Rancheros means "Rancher's Eggs" in Spanish and is a hearty breakfast dish popular in Mexico.

2 servings   400 cal   20 min

French Toast with Maple Syrup

A sweet and satisfying breakfast with crispy French toast and drizzled maple syrup.

Ingredients:

- 4 slices of bread
- 2 large eggs
- 1/2 cup milk
- 1/2 tsp vanilla extract
- Butter for frying
- Maple syrup for topping

Directions

1. In a bowl, whisk eggs, milk, and vanilla extract.
2. Heat a pan with butter over medium heat.
3. Dip bread slices into the egg mixture and fry until golden.
4. Serve with maple syrup.

Fun Facts

French toast has been enjoyed since at least the 4th century and is known by various names in different cultures.

1 omelette   280 cal   15 min

Western-Style Omelette

A hearty omelette filled with ham, bell peppers, onions, and cheese.

Ingredients:

- 3 large eggs
- 1/4 cup diced ham
- 1/4 cup diced bell peppers
- 1/4 cup diced onions
- 1/4 cup shredded cheddar cheese
- Salt and pepper, to taste

Directions

1. Beat eggs in a bowl and add salt and pepper.
2. Heat a pan over medium heat and add ham, peppers, and onions. Cook until tender.
3. Pour beaten eggs into the pan and cook until set.
4. Sprinkle cheese and fold omelette in half. Serve hot.

Fun Facts

The Western omelette, also known as a Denver omelette, likely originated in the western United States.

2 servings   350 cal   30 min

Creamy Polenta with Fried Eggs

Creamy polenta topped with sunny-side-up eggs, a hearty Italian breakfast.

Ingredients:

- 1 cup cornmeal
- 4 cups water
- 1/2 cup grated Parmesan cheese
- 4 large eggs
- Salt and pepper, to taste

Directions

1. Bring water to a boil in a saucepan.
2. Gradually whisk in cornmeal and cook until creamy.
3. Stir in Parmesan cheese, season with salt and pepper.
4. In a separate pan, fry eggs sunny side up.
5. Serve polenta with fried eggs on top.

Fun Facts

Polenta is a traditional Italian dish made from ground cornmeal, similar to grits in the American South.

Chapter 2:
Creative Egg Brunches

2 servings | 380 cal | 15 min

Smoked Salmon and Egg Bagel

A sophisticated brunch with luscious smoked salmon and creamy eggs on a toasted bagel.

Ingredients:

- 2 large eggs
- 2 bagels
- 4 oz smoked salmon
- 2 tbsp cream cheese
- Capers and red onion slices for garnish

Directions

1. Toast the bagels until golden.
2. Spread cream cheese on each half.
3. Layer smoked salmon on one half.
4. Fry eggs sunny side up and place on the salmon.
5. Garnish with capers and red onion slices. Serve open-faced.

Fun Facts

Smoked salmon is often associated with luxury and is a favorite addition to many upscale brunch dishes.

4 servings

320 cal

30 min

Asparagus and Goat Cheese Frittata

An elegant frittata featuring tender asparagus spears and creamy goat cheese.

Ingredients:

- 8 large eggs
- 1 bunch asparagus, trimmed and cut into 2-inch pieces
- 1/2 cup crumbled goat cheese
- Salt and pepper, to taste

Directions

1. Preheat the broiler.
2. In an oven-safe skillet, sauté asparagus until tender.
3. Beat eggs, season with salt and pepper, and pour over asparagus.
4. Cook on the stovetop until edges set, then transfer to the broiler to finish.
5. Sprinkle goat cheese and broil until golden. Slice and serve.

Fun Facts

Frittata is an Italian egg dish, similar to an omelette, that can be customized with various ingredients.

2 servings | 420 cal | 20 min

Avocado and Egg Breakfast Burrito

Easy

A hearty breakfast burrito filled with creamy avocado, eggs, and salsa.

Ingredients:

- 4 large eggs
- 2 large tortillas
- 1 ripe avocado, sliced
- 1/2 cup salsa
- Salt and pepper, to taste

Directions

1. Scramble eggs and season with salt and pepper.
2. Warm tortillas in a dry pan or microwave.
3. Lay avocado slices on each tortilla.
4. Add scrambled eggs and salsa.
5. Roll up and serve.

Fun Facts

Avocado adds a creamy and nutritious twist to breakfast burritos, providing healthy fats and a velvety texture.

4 servings   290 cal   40 min

Spinach and Mushroom Quiche

A savory quiche filled with sautéed spinach, mushrooms, and a flaky pastry crust.

Ingredients:

- 4 large eggs
- 1 9-inch pie crust (store-bought or homemade)
- 1 cup fresh spinach, chopped
- 1 cup sliced mushrooms
- 1/2 cup shredded Swiss cheese
- 1/2 cup heavy cream
- Salt and pepper, to taste

Directions

1. Preheat the oven to 375°F (190°C).
2. Sautee spinach and mushrooms until tender.
3. In a bowl, whisk eggs, cream, salt, and pepper.
4. Place the sautéed vegetables and Swiss cheese in the pie crust.
5. Pour the egg mixture over the filling.
6. Bake for 30-35 minutes until set and lightly browned. Slice and serve.

Fun Facts

Quiche is a French dish that originated in the medieval German kingdom of Lothringen, which the French later renamed Lorraine.

6 muffins | 200 cal | 25 min

Cheddar and Chive Egg Muffins

Cheesy, savory muffins loaded with cheddar, fresh chives, and fluffy scrambled eggs.

Ingredients:

- 6 large eggs
- 1/2 cup grated cheddar cheese
- 2 tbsp chopped fresh chives
- 1/4 cup milk
- Salt and pepper, to taste

Directions

1. Preheat the oven to 375°F (190°C) and grease a muffin tin.
2. Whisk eggs, milk, cheddar, chives, salt, and pepper in a bowl.
3. Pour the mixture into the muffin cups.
4. Bake for 20-25 minutes until set and golden brown.

Fun Facts

Muffins for breakfast? Yes, please! These savory muffins are a delightful twist on the classic breakfast.

2 servings   420 cal   30 min

Breakfast Pizza with Sunny-Side-Up Eggs

A delicious breakfast pizza topped with crispy bacon, mozzarella, and perfectly cooked sunny-side-up eggs.

Ingredients:

- 2 large pizza crusts (store-bought or homemade)
- 4 large eggs
- 4 slices of cooked bacon, crumbled
- 1 cup shredded mozzarella cheese
- Salt and pepper, to taste

Directions

1. Preheat the oven to 425°F (220°C).
2. Place pizza crusts on a baking sheet.
3. Sprinkle mozzarella cheese and bacon on each crust.
4. Create a well in the center for each egg.
5. Crack an egg into each well.
6. Season with salt and pepper.
7. Bake for 15-20 minutes until the crust is golden and eggs are set.

Fun Facts

Breakfast pizza is a creative twist on a classic Italian favorite, perfect for brunch or anytime.

2 servings 320 cal 20 min

Eggs in Purgatory

A spicy and flavorful dish where eggs are poached in a fiery tomato sauce.

Ingredients:

- 4 large eggs
- 2 cups tomato sauce
- 1/2 tsp red pepper flakes
- 1/4 cup grated Parmesan cheese
- Salt and pepper, to taste

Directions

1. Heat tomato sauce in a skillet, add red pepper flakes, and season with salt and pepper.
2. Make small wells in the sauce and crack eggs into them.
3. Cover and poach until the eggs are cooked to your liking.
4. Sprinkle with Parmesan cheese. Serve with crusty bread.

Fun Facts

"Eggs in Purgatory" is also known as "Uova in Purgatorio" in Italian, and it's a fiery and flavorful dish.

4 servings   **280 cal**   **30 min**

Sweet Potato and Egg Hash

A hearty and wholesome hash with sweet potatoes, bell peppers, and sunny-side-up eggs.

Ingredients:

- 4 large eggs
- 2 sweet potatoes, peeled and diced
- 1 red bell pepper, diced
- 1/2 onion, chopped
- 2 tbsp olive oil
- Salt and pepper, to taste

Directions

1. Heat olive oil in a skillet over medium heat.
2. Add sweet potatoes and cook until tender and golden.
3. Add bell pepper and onion, sauté until soft.
4. Create wells in the hash and crack eggs into them.
5. Cover and cook until the eggs are set. Serve hot.

Fun Facts

Hash is a versatile dish made with diced potatoes and a variety of ingredients, often served for breakfast or brunch.

2 servings   340 cal   25 min

Eggs Florentine

A classic brunch dish with poached eggs and creamy spinach sauce on toasted English muffins.

Ingredients:

- 4 large eggs
- 2 English muffins
- 2 cups fresh spinach
- 1/2 cup heavy cream
- 1/4 cup grated Parmesan cheese
- Salt and pepper, to taste

Directions

1. Toast the English muffins and keep warm.
2. In a saucepan, wilt spinach, add heavy cream, Parmesan cheese, salt, and pepper.
3. Poach eggs to your desired doneness.
4. Place spinach sauce on each muffin half, top with a poached egg. Serve hot.

Fun Facts

"Eggs Florentine" is named after Florence, Italy, and is a popular variant of the classic Eggs Benedict.

2 servings | 420 cal | 30 min

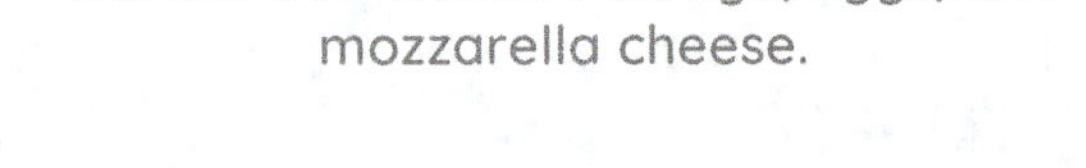

Italian Sausage and Egg Calzone

A savory and satisfying breakfast calzone stuffed with Italian sausage, eggs, and mozzarella cheese.

Ingredients:

- 4 large eggs
- 8 oz Italian sausage, cooked and crumbled
- 1 cup shredded mozzarella cheese
- 2 pizza dough rounds (store-bought or homemade)
- Salt and pepper, to taste

Directions

1. Preheat the oven to 400°F (200°C).
2. Roll out pizza dough rounds into circles.
3. On one half of each dough, add sausage, eggs, and mozzarella cheese.
4. Fold the other half over and seal the edges.
5. Bake for 20-25 minutes until golden brown. Slice and serve.

Fun Facts

Calzones are a popular Italian snack, often filled with various ingredients, making them perfect for customization.

Chapter 3:
International Egg Delights

4 pieces   180 cal   40 min

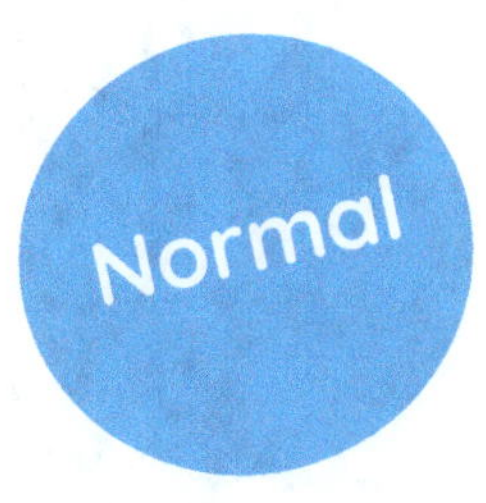

Japanese Tamago Sushi

Sweet and fluffy Japanese omelet sushi, a delightful sushi variation.

Ingredients:

- 4 sheets of nori (seaweed)
- 1 cup sushi rice
- 4 eggs
- 2 tbsp sugar
- 2 tbsp soy sauce
- Salt and vegetable oil for cooking

Directions

1. Cook sushi rice and let it cool.
2. Beat eggs, sugar, soy sauce, and a pinch of salt.
3. Heat a non-stick pan and lightly oil it.
4. Pour a thin layer of egg mixture, cook, and roll it up.
5. Slice into strips and set aside.
6. Place nori on a bamboo sushi rolling mat, spread rice, and arrange egg strips.
7. Roll up tightly and slice into 4 pieces.

Fun Facts

Tamago sushi is a staple in Japanese cuisine, often enjoyed in sushi bars and bento boxes.

4 servings | 350 cal | 30 min

Indian Masala Egg Curry

A rich and flavorful Indian curry with hard-boiled eggs in a spiced tomato sauce.

Ingredients:

- 4 hard-boiled eggs, peeled
- 2 onions, finely chopped
- 2 tomatoes, pureed
- 2 cloves garlic, minced
- 1-inch ginger, grated
- 1/2 cup yogurt
- 2 tsp garam masala
- 1 tsp turmeric
- 1 tsp cumin
- Salt and vegetable oil for cooking

Directions

1. Heat oil in a pan, add chopped onions, and sauté until golden.
2. Add garlic, ginger, and spices, and cook until fragrant.
3. Stir in tomato puree and simmer for a few minutes.
4. Add yogurt and simmer until the oil separates.
5. Add hard-boiled eggs and cook until heated through. Serve with rice or bread.

Fun Facts

"Masala" refers to a blend of spices in Indian cuisine, and this curry is a flavorful favorite.

2 servings | 420 cal | 25 min

Mexican Chilaquiles

A hearty Mexican dish made with crispy tortilla chips, eggs, and spicy salsa.

Ingredients:

- 4 cups tortilla chips
- 4 large eggs
- 1 cup red or green salsa
- 1/2 cup crumbled queso fresco
- Chopped cilantro and sliced red onion for garnish

Directions

1. Heat salsa in a pan until simmering.
2. Add tortilla chips and stir to coat.
3. Create small wells in the chips and crack eggs into them.
4. Cover and cook until the eggs are set.
5. Garnish with queso fresco, cilantro, and sliced red onion.

Fun Facts

Chilaquiles are a popular Mexican breakfast dish, often served with a variety of toppings and salsas.

2 servings   320 cal   30 min

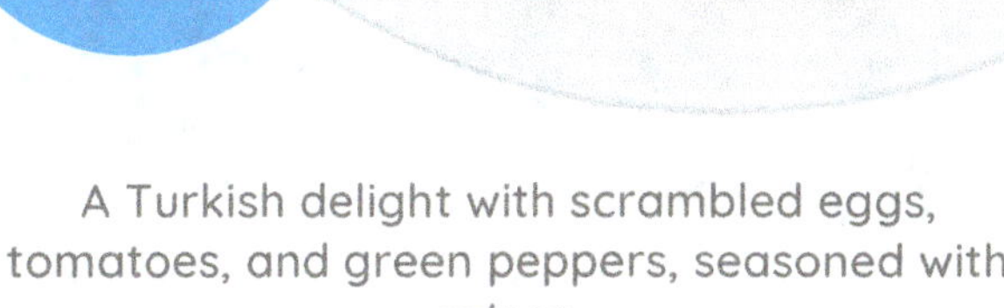

Turkish Menemen

A Turkish delight with scrambled eggs, tomatoes, and green peppers, seasoned with spices.

Ingredients:

- 4 large eggs
- 2 tomatoes, diced
- 2 green peppers, diced
- 1 onion, chopped
- 2 cloves garlic, minced
- 2 tbsp olive oil
- 1 tsp red pepper flakes
- Salt and pepper, to taste

Directions

1. Heat olive oil in a pan, add onions and peppers, and sauté until soft.
2. Add garlic, tomatoes, and spices, and cook until tomatoes break down.
3. Beat eggs and pour over the mixture.
4. Scramble until cooked to your liking. Serve hot.

Fun Facts

Menemen is a classic Turkish dish often served as a hearty breakfast or brunch.

4 servings | 300 cal | 25 min

Chinese Egg Fried Rice

Easy

A classic Chinese dish with fluffy fried rice, eggs, and a medley of vegetables.

Ingredients:

- 2 cups cooked and cooled rice
- 4 large eggs
- 1 cup mixed vegetables (peas, carrots, corn)
- 2 cloves garlic, minced
- 2 tbsp soy sauce
- 2 tbsp vegetable oil
- Salt and pepper, to taste

Directions

1. Heat vegetable oil in a wok or large pan.
2. Add minced garlic and stir-fry until fragrant.
3. Push the garlic to the side and scramble the eggs in the wok.
4. Add mixed vegetables and stir-fry until tender.
5. Add rice and soy sauce, stir-fry until well combined and heated through.

Fun Facts

Egg fried rice is a popular Chinese takeout dish that you can easily make at home.

4 servings | 290 cal | 40 min

Greek Spanakopita

A Greek pastry filled with spinach and feta cheese, featuring layers of flaky phyllo dough.

Ingredients:

- 8 sheets phyllo dough
- 4 large eggs
- 2 cups fresh spinach, chopped
- 1 cup crumbled feta cheese
- 1/2 cup chopped green onions
- 2 tbsp olive oil
- Salt and pepper, to taste

Directions

1. Preheat the oven to 350°F (175°C).
2. In a bowl, beat eggs, stir in spinach, feta, green onions, salt, and pepper.
3. Brush a baking dish with olive oil, layer phyllo dough sheets, brushing each layer with more oil.
4. Spread the spinach and egg mixture on top.
5. Fold the overhanging dough over the filling and bake for 30-35 minutes until golden.

Fun Facts

Spanakopita is a traditional Greek dish that's often served as an appetizer or snack.

2 servings   340 cal   30 min

Lebanese Shakshuka

A Middle Eastern breakfast dish with poached eggs in a spicy tomato and bell pepper sauce.

Ingredients:

- 4 large eggs
- 2 tomatoes, diced
- 2 red bell peppers, diced
- 1 onion, chopped
- 2 cloves garlic, minced
- 2 tbsp olive oil
- 1 tsp cumin
- 1 tsp paprika
- Salt and pepper, to taste

Directions

1. Heat olive oil in a skillet, add onions, and sauté until soft.
2. Add garlic, bell peppers, and spices, and cook until peppers are tender.
3. Stir in diced tomatoes and simmer until the sauce thickens.
4. Make small wells in the sauce and crack eggs into them.
5. Cover and poach until the eggs are set. Serve with crusty bread.

Fun Facts

Shakshuka is a popular dish in many Middle Eastern and North African countries, each with its own variation.

2 servings   400 cal   35 min

Korean Bibimbap with Fried Egg

A Korean rice dish with assorted vegetables, marinated beef, and a crispy fried egg on top.

Ingredients:

- 2 cups cooked rice
- 4 oz thinly sliced beef (marinated)
- 2 large eggs
- Assorted vegetables (e.g., spinach, bean sprouts, carrots)
- Gochujang (Korean chili paste)
- Sesame oil and soy sauce for seasoning
- Salt and vegetable oil for cooking

Directions

1. Cook rice and set aside.
2. Stir-fry marinated beef and set aside.
3. Cook assorted vegetables and season with sesame oil and soy sauce.
4. Fry eggs sunny side up.
5. Assemble bibimbap by placing rice, beef, vegetables, and a fried egg on top.
6. Serve with gochujang on the side.

Fun Facts

Bibimbap is a popular Korean rice dish known for its vibrant colors and unique mix of flavors and textures.

4 servings   350 cal   35 min

Spanish Tortilla Espanola

Easy

A classic Spanish dish with potatoes and onions, bound together with eggs and pan-fried to perfection.

Ingredients:

- 4 large eggs
- 2 potatoes, peeled and thinly sliced
- 1 onion, thinly sliced
- Olive oil for frying
- Salt and pepper, to taste

Directions

1. Heat olive oil in a skillet and add potatoes and onions.
2. Cook until potatoes are tender and onions are soft.
3. Beat eggs, season with salt and pepper, and pour over the potatoes and onions.
4. Cook until set on the bottom, then flip and cook the other side until golden. Serve hot or at room temperature.

Fun Facts

Tortilla Española is a staple in Spanish cuisine, often served as tapas or in a sandwich.

Chapter 4:
Egg Appetizers and Small Bites

12 pieces   180 cal   20 min

Deviled Eggs with Bacon

Classic deviled eggs with a twist, garnished with crispy bacon.

Ingredients:

- 6 large eggs
- 3 strips of crispy bacon, crumbled
- 2 tbsp mayonnaise
- 1 tsp Dijon mustard
- Salt, pepper, and paprika to taste

Directions

1. Hard-boil eggs, cool, peel, and cut in half.
2. Remove yolks and mash them with mayo, mustard, salt, pepper.
3. Spoon mixture back into egg whites.
4. Garnish with crumbled bacon and a sprinkle of paprika. Serve chilled.

Fun Facts

Deviled eggs are believed to have originated in ancient Rome, and variations exist in many cultures.

4 servings   350 cal   30 min

Scotch Eggs

A British pub favorite featuring hard-boiled eggs encased in sausage meat and breadcrumbs.

Ingredients:

- 4 hard-boiled eggs, peeled
- 1/2 lb ground sausage meat
- 1 cup breadcrumbs
- 1/4 cup flour
- 1 egg, beaten
- Salt and pepper, to taste

Directions

1. Coat eggs in seasoned flour, then wrap them in a layer of sausage meat.
2. Dip in beaten egg, then roll in breadcrumbs.
3. Heat oil in a pan and fry the coated eggs until golden and sausage is cooked.
4. Slice and serve hot or cold.

Fun Facts

Scotch eggs are named after a snack popular in 19th-century England, which was meant to be portable and easy to eat.

12 pieces   **240 cal**   **35 min**

Mini Quiches with Spinach

Bite-sized quiches with a flaky crust, filled with spinach and creamy egg custard.

Ingredients:

- 1 pie crust, store-bought or homemade
- 4 large eggs
- 1 cup chopped fresh spinach
- 1/2 cup shredded Gruyère cheese
- 1/2 cup heavy cream
- Salt, pepper, and nutmeg to taste

Directions

1. Preheat the oven to 350°F (175°C).
2. Roll out the pie crust and cut into rounds to fit a muffin tin.
3. In a bowl, whisk eggs, cream, cheese, spinach, and seasonings.
4. Pour the mixture into the crusts.
5. Bake for 20-25 minutes until set and golden.

Fun Facts

Quiches originated in Germany and are known for their buttery crust and creamy egg filling.

12 pieces   200 cal   25 min

Smoked Salmon Deviled Eggs

Deviled eggs with a luxurious twist, featuring the delicate flavor of smoked salmon.

Ingredients:

- 6 large eggs
- 2 oz smoked salmon, finely chopped
- 2 tbsp mayonnaise
- 1 tsp Dijon mustard
- Fresh dill, for garnish
- Salt, pepper, and paprika to taste

Directions

1. Hard-boil eggs, cool, peel, and cut in half.
2. Remove yolks and mash them with mayo, mustard, salt, pepper.
3. Stir in chopped smoked salmon.
4. Spoon mixture back into egg whites.
5. Garnish with fresh dill and a sprinkle of paprika. Serve chilled.

Fun Facts

Smoked salmon is often considered a delicacy, known for its rich and smoky flavor.

6 servings   150 cal   15 min

Tangy and colorful pickled eggs, perfect as a quick and zesty appetizer.

Pickled Eggs

Ingredients:

- 6 large hard-boiled eggs
- 1 cup vinegar
- 1/2 cup water
- 1/4 cup sugar
- 1/2 tsp pickling spices
- Salt and pepper, to taste

Directions

1. Peel hard-boiled eggs and place them in a jar.
2. In a saucepan, heat vinegar, water, sugar, spices, salt, and pepper until sugar dissolves.
3. Pour the liquid over the eggs in the jar.
4. Seal the jar and refrigerate for at least 24 hours before serving.

Fun Facts

Pickled eggs are a popular bar snack and can be customized with various seasonings and spices.

12 pieces | 250 cal | 20 min

Avocado and Egg Canapés

Elegant canapés featuring creamy avocado, a slice of boiled egg, and a sprinkle of paprika.

Ingredients:

- 6 large eggs
- 1 ripe avocado
- 1 lemon, juiced
- Salt, pepper, and paprika to taste
- 12 small slices of baguette or crackers

Directions

1. Hard-boil eggs, cool, peel, and slice into 12 rounds.
2. Mash the ripe avocado with lemon juice, salt, and pepper.
3. Spread the avocado mixture on baguette slices.
4. Top each with a slice of boiled egg and a sprinkle of paprika. Serve chilled.

Fun Facts

Canapés are small, bite-sized appetizers that are often served at upscale events and gatherings.

12 pieces   300 cal   25 min

Bacon-Wrapped Egg Bites

Savory bites featuring eggs wrapped in crispy bacon, a perfect combination of flavors and textures.

Ingredients:

- 6 large eggs
- 6 slices of bacon
- Salt, pepper, and chives for garnish

Directions

1. Preheat the oven to 350°F (175°C).
2. Partially cook bacon slices until they are still pliable but not crispy.
3. Line a muffin tin with bacon slices, creating a "cup" for the egg.
4. Crack an egg into each bacon cup, season with salt and pepper.
5. Bake for 15-20 minutes until the eggs are set and bacon is crispy. Garnish with chives.

Fun Facts

Bacon-wrapped bites are a crowd-pleasing favorite at parties and brunches.

4 servings   280 cal   30 min

Prosciutto-Wrapped Asparagus with Poached Egg

An elegant appetizer featuring tender asparagus spears, prosciutto, and a perfectly poached egg.

Ingredients:

- 1 lb asparagus spears
- 4 large eggs
- 4 slices prosciutto
- 1 tbsp white vinegar
- Salt and pepper, to taste

Directions

1. Blanch asparagus in boiling water, then shock in ice water to preserve the color.
2. Wrap each asparagus bundle with a slice of prosciutto.
3. Poach eggs until the whites are set but yolks are still runny.
4. Place an asparagus bundle on each plate and top with a poached egg.
5. Season with salt and pepper.

Fun Facts

Asparagus and poached eggs are a classic combination, often enjoyed in various cuisines.

12 pieces | 220 cal | 30 min

Egg-Stuffed Mushrooms

Savory stuffed mushrooms filled with a delightful mixture of eggs and herbs.

Ingredients:

- 12 large mushrooms
- 2 large eggs
- 1/2 cup breadcrumbs
- 1/4 cup grated Parmesan cheese
- 2 cloves garlic, minced
- Fresh herbs (e.g., parsley, thyme)
- Salt and pepper, to taste

Directions

1. Remove stems from mushrooms and chop them.
2. In a bowl, combine chopped stems, eggs, breadcrumbs, Parmesan, garlic, herbs, salt, and pepper.
3. Stuff each mushroom cap with the mixture.
4. Bake in a preheated oven at 375°F (190°C) for 20-25 minutes.

Fun Facts

Stuffed mushrooms are a versatile appetizer, and you can customize the filling with various ingredients.

12 pieces | 320 cal | 40 min

Egg and Caviar Blinis

Luxurious blinis topped with soft-boiled eggs, creme fraiche, and a dollop of caviar.

Ingredients:

- 6 large eggs
- 12 mini blinis (store-bought or homemade)
- 1/2 cup creme fraiche
- 2 oz caviar
- Fresh chives, for garnish
- Salt and pepper, to taste

Directions

1. Soft-boil eggs, cool, peel, and slice in half.
2. Spread creme fraiche on each blini.
3. Top with a slice of soft-boiled egg, a dollop of caviar, and a sprinkle of salt, pepper, and fresh chives. Serve chilled.

Fun Facts

Caviar is a delicacy known for its exquisite taste and is often enjoyed on special occasions.

We have a small favor to ask

Midway through our journey of mastering the art of eggs in the "Best of Eggs Cookbook: Crack & Cook" with over 100 delectable creations, I'd like to take a brief pause, not to crack a joke, but to crack a sincere request.

Reviews, my fellow egg enthusiasts, are like the perfectly poached egg—subtle yet transformative. For small publishers like us, they are the golden yolk that brightens our culinary path.

If you could spare a moment, kindly venture back to the platform where you discovered this eggstravaganza—whether it's an app or an online marketplace. There, amidst the sea of choices, you'll find the review button. We would be immensely grateful if you could bless us with your honest rating and a concise, flavorful sentence capturing your egg-citing journey so far.

Every review is a whisk of encouragement for us. They're the secret ingredient that makes our cookbook truly scramble-free, and they mean more than the perfect runny yolk on a sunny morning. In the spirit of full disclosure, should you come across a minor hiccup within these pages, please know we've tried to whip up perfection. We're not infallible, and, much like a slightly overcooked omelette, small mistakes can happen. We hope you can savor the overall egg-citing experience despite these minor imperfections.

Your support, conveyed through a review, is like the perfect flip of an omelette—it completes the egg experience and inspires us to keep cracking delightful recipes. So, without further ado, let's return to the recipes and continue our journey of mastering the extraordinary world of eggs. With sincere gratitude and a sprinkle of salt, let the eggstravaganza continue!

Chapter 5:
Hearty Egg Lunches

2 servings 340 cal 20 min

Egg Salad Sandwich

A classic sandwich featuring creamy egg salad with a hint of mustard.

Ingredients:

- 4 large eggs
- 2 tbsp mayonnaise
- 1 tsp Dijon mustard
- Salt, pepper, and paprika to taste
- Slices of bread
- Lettuce and tomato for garnish

Directions

1. Hard-boil eggs, cool, peel, and chop them.
2. In a bowl, mix chopped eggs with mayonnaise, mustard, salt, pepper, and paprika.
3. Spread the egg salad on slices of bread.
4. Add lettuce and tomato slices. Assemble into sandwiches.

Fun Facts

Egg salad sandwiches are a timeless favorite, often enjoyed for their simple yet satisfying flavor.

2 servings 420 cal 20 min

Avocado and Egg BLT

A modern twist on the classic BLT, featuring creamy avocado and a fried egg.

Ingredients:

- 4 slices of bacon
- 2 large eggs
- 1 avocado, sliced
- Slices of bread
- Lettuce, tomato, and mayonnaise for garnish

Directions

1. Cook bacon until crispy, then drain on paper towels.
2. In the same pan, fry eggs sunny side up.
3. Toast slices of bread and spread with mayonnaise.
4. Assemble sandwiches with bacon, lettuce, tomato, avocado, and a fried egg.

Fun Facts

The BLT is a classic American sandwich, known for its combination of bacon, lettuce, and tomato.

2 servings — 380 cal — 20 min

Ramen with Soft-Boiled Egg

Comforting ramen noodles in a flavorful broth, topped with a soft-boiled egg.

Ingredients:

- 2 packs of ramen noodles
- 2 large eggs
- 4 cups chicken or vegetable broth
- Sliced green onions and sesame seeds for garnish
- Soy sauce and hot sauce, to taste

Directions

1. Cook ramen noodles according to the package instructions and drain.
2. In a separate pot, heat the broth until it's simmering.
3. Soft-boil eggs and slice them in half.
4. Divide cooked noodles into two bowls and pour hot broth over them.
5. Top with a soft-boiled egg, green onions, sesame seeds, soy sauce, and hot sauce.

Fun Facts

Soft-boiled eggs are a popular ramen topping, known for their creamy yolk and comforting texture.

2 servings

350 cal

25 min

Cobb Salad with Hard-Boiled Eggs

A hearty salad featuring crispy bacon, hard-boiled eggs, and creamy blue cheese dressing.

Ingredients:

- 4 cups mixed salad greens
- 4 large eggs
- 4 strips of bacon, cooked and crumbled
- 1 cup diced cooked chicken
- 1/2 cup crumbled blue cheese
- Cherry tomatoes, sliced avocado, and red onion for garnish
- Blue cheese dressing

Directions

1. Hard-boil eggs, cool, peel, and slice them.
2. In a bowl, arrange salad greens, bacon, chicken, blue cheese, cherry tomatoes, avocado, and red onion.
3. Top with sliced hard-boiled eggs.
4. Drizzle with blue cheese dressing.

Fun Facts

The Cobb salad is a classic American salad, named after Robert Cobb, who created it in the 1930s.

4 servings   320 cal   35 min

Broccoli and Cheddar Egg Bake

A savory egg bake with broccoli and cheddar cheese, perfect for a filling lunch.

Ingredients:

- 8 large eggs
- 2 cups chopped broccoli
- 1 cup shredded cheddar cheese
- 1/2 cup milk
- 1/2 cup diced onion
- 2 cloves garlic, minced
- Salt and pepper, to taste

Directions

1. Preheat the oven to 350°F (175°C).
2. In a bowl, beat eggs, milk, cheese, onion, garlic, salt, and pepper.
3. Grease a baking dish, spread broccoli evenly, and pour the egg mixture over it.
4. Bake for 25-30 minutes until the eggs are set and the top is golden.

Fun Facts

Egg bakes are versatile dishes that can be customized with a variety of ingredients.

2 servings   360 cal   20 min

Mediterranean Egg Wrap

A Mediterranean-inspired wrap with scrambled eggs, feta cheese, and fresh herbs.

Ingredients:

- 4 large eggs
- 1/2 cup crumbled feta cheese
- Fresh parsley and dill, chopped
- 2 whole-wheat tortillas
- Sliced cucumber, tomato, and olives for garnish
- Olive oil for drizzling

Directions

1. Scramble eggs until cooked to your liking, then stir in feta, parsley, and dill.
2. Warm tortillas in a dry skillet.
3. Divide the egg mixture between the tortillas.
4. Top with cucumber, tomato, and olives.
5. Drizzle with olive oil and fold the tortillas to make wraps.

Fun Facts

Mediterranean cuisine is known for its use of fresh herbs, olive oil, and simple yet flavorful ingredients.

2 servings | 400 cal | 25 min

Tuna and Egg Niçoise Salad

A French classic salad with tuna, hard-boiled eggs, green beans, and olives.

Ingredients:

- 2 large eggs
- 2 cans of tuna, drained
- 2 cups cooked green beans
- Cherry tomatoes and Kalamata olives
- Mixed salad greens
- Olive oil and Dijon mustard for dressing

Directions

1. Hard-boil eggs, cool, peel, and slice them.
2. Arrange mixed salad greens, tuna, green beans, cherry tomatoes, olives, and sliced hard-boiled eggs on plates.
3. In a bowl, whisk olive oil and Dijon mustard to make a dressing.
4. Drizzle dressing over the salad.

Fun Facts

The Niçoise salad is named after the city of Nice in the south of France, known for its fresh and vibrant flavors.

2 servings 350 cal 25 min

Spicy Kimchi Fried Rice with Egg

A Korean-inspired fried rice dish with spicy kimchi and a sunny-side-up egg.

Ingredients:

- 2 cups cooked and cooled rice
- 2 large eggs
- 1 cup chopped kimchi
- 2 cloves garlic, minced
- 2 green onions, chopped
- 2 tbsp gochujang (Korean chili paste)
- Soy sauce and sesame oil, to taste

Directions

1. Heat a pan with oil, add garlic, and sauté until fragrant.
2. Stir in chopped kimchi and gochujang, cooking for a few minutes.
3. Add rice and mix well.
4. Make a well in the rice, crack an egg into it, and cook until the whites are set but the yolk is still runny.
5. Top with green onions and season with soy sauce and sesame oil.

Fun Facts

Kimchi is a popular Korean side dish made from fermented vegetables, often used to add flavor and spice to dishes.

4 servings   320 cal   40 min

Quinoa and Egg Stuffed Peppers

Bell peppers stuffed with a mixture of quinoa, vegetables, and a baked egg on top.

Ingredients:

- 4 large bell peppers
- 4 large eggs
- 1 cup cooked quinoa
- 1/2 cup diced tomatoes
- 1/2 cup diced bell pepper
- 1/4 cup diced red onion
- 1/4 cup grated cheddar cheese
- Salt and pepper, to taste

Directions

1. Preheat the oven to 375°F (190°C).
2. Cut the tops off the bell peppers and remove the seeds.
3. In a bowl, mix quinoa, diced tomatoes, diced bell pepper, diced red onion, cheddar cheese, salt, and pepper.
4. Fill each bell pepper with the quinoa mixture.
5. Crack an egg on top of each stuffed pepper.
6. Bake for 25-30 minutes until the egg whites are set but the yolks are still runny.

Fun Facts

Stuffed peppers are a versatile dish that can be filled with a variety of ingredients, making them a go-to comfort food.

2 servings   380 cal   20 min

Egg and Roasted Red Pepper Panini

A panini featuring roasted red peppers, sliced egg, mozzarella cheese, and basil.

Ingredients:

- 4 slices of ciabatta bread
- 2 large eggs
- 1 roasted red pepper, sliced
- 4 slices of mozzarella cheese
- Fresh basil leaves
- Olive oil for grilling

Directions

1. Preheat a panini press or grill pan.
2. Grill the ciabatta slices until they have grill marks.
3. Fry or poach eggs sunny side up.
4. Assemble sandwiches with roasted red pepper, mozzarella, basil, and a fried or poached egg between grilled bread slices.
5. Press in the panini press or grill until the cheese is melted.

Fun Facts

Paninis are Italian sandwiches that are typically grilled and pressed, creating a warm and crispy texture.

Chapter 6:
Egg Dinner Delicacies

4 servings | 450 cal | 30 min

Classic Beef Stroganoff with Egg Noodles

A comforting Russian dish featuring tender strips of beef in a creamy mushroom sauce, served over egg noodles.

Ingredients:

- 1 lb beef sirloin, thinly sliced
- 1 onion, chopped
- 8 oz mushrooms, sliced
- 2 cloves garlic, minced
- 1 cup sour cream
- 2 tbsp flour
- 2 cups beef broth
- 1 tbsp Dijon mustard
- Egg noodles
- Fresh parsley for garnish

Directions

1. In a pan, heat oil and cook beef until browned. Remove from pan and set aside.
2. In the same pan, sauté onions and mushrooms until tender.
3. Stir in garlic and flour, then add beef broth and mustard.
4. Return beef to the pan and simmer until the sauce thickens.
5. Stir in sour cream and heat through.
6. Cook egg noodles according to the package instructions and serve beef stroganoff over them. Garnish with fresh parsley.

Fun Facts

Beef Stroganoff is believed to have been named after a Russian diplomat, Count Pavel Stroganov.

4 servings   380 cal   35 min

Thai Green Curry with Poached Eggs

A fragrant Thai green curry with vegetables and tender poached eggs.

Ingredients:

- 4 large eggs
- 1 can of green curry paste
- 1 can of coconut milk
- Assorted vegetables (e.g., bell peppers, zucchini, and carrots)
- Fresh basil leaves and lime wedges for garnish

Directions

1. In a pot, heat green curry paste and coconut milk until it simmers.
2. Add assorted vegetables and simmer until tender.
3. Poach eggs in the curry until the whites are set but the yolks are still runny.
4. Serve with fresh basil leaves and lime wedges.

Fun Facts

Thai green curry is known for its aromatic blend of herbs and spices, creating a flavorful and spicy dish.

4 servings **320 cal** **40 min**

Korean Japchae with Egg Ribbons

A Korean stir-fried noodle dish with colorful vegetables and delicate egg ribbons.

Ingredients:

- 4 large eggs
- 8 oz Korean glass noodles (dangmyeon)
- Assorted vegetables (e.g., bell peppers, carrots, spinach)
- Soy sauce, sugar, and sesame oil for seasoning
- Sesame seeds for garnish

Directions

1. Soak glass noodles in warm water until they soften, then drain.
2. In a pan, stir-fry vegetables and glass noodles with soy sauce, sugar, and sesame oil until tender.
3. Create thin egg ribbons by beating eggs and pouring them into a hot, oiled pan like a crepe.
4. Slice the egg ribbons and mix them into the japchae.
5. Garnish with sesame seeds.

Fun Facts

Japchae is a popular Korean dish often served at special occasions, known for its sweet and savory flavors.

4 servings   300 cal   30 min

Chinese Sweet and Sour Eggs

A sweet and tangy Chinese dish with eggs poached in a flavorful sauce.

Ingredients:

- 4 large eggs
- 1/2 cup vinegar
- 1/2 cup sugar
- 1/2 cup ketchup
- 1/4 cup water
- Salt and pepper, to taste

Directions

1. Hard-boil eggs, cool, peel, and slice them.
2. In a pot, combine vinegar, sugar, ketchup, water, salt, and pepper.
3. Simmer the sauce until it thickens.
4. Add the sliced eggs and heat through.
5. Serve hot, with steamed rice if desired.

Fun Facts

Sweet and sour dishes are a common theme in Chinese cuisine, known for their contrast of flavors.

4 servings | 380 cal | 25 min

Italian Carbonara

A classic Italian pasta dish with a creamy sauce made from eggs, cheese, and pancetta.

Ingredients:

- 8 oz spaghetti
- 4 large eggs
- 1 cup grated Pecorino Romano cheese
- 4 oz pancetta or guanciale
- Black pepper and salt, to taste

Directions

1. Cook spaghetti according to package instructions until al dente, then drain.
2. In a bowl, whisk eggs, grated cheese, and black pepper.
3. In a pan, cook pancetta until crispy.
4. Toss cooked spaghetti in the pan with the pancetta.
5. Remove from heat and quickly stir in the egg and cheese mixture.
6. The heat from the pasta will create a creamy sauce. Season with salt and additional cheese if desired.

Fun Facts

Carbonara is a Roman pasta dish known for its simplicity and richness, made with basic ingredients.

4 servings | 420 cal | 40 min

Eggplant Parmesan

A hearty Italian dish with breaded and fried eggplant slices, topped with tomato sauce and melted cheese.

Ingredients:

- 2 large eggplants, sliced
- 4 large eggs
- 1 cup breadcrumbs
- 1 cup grated Parmesan cheese
- 2 cups marinara sauce
- 2 cups shredded mozzarella cheese
- Fresh basil leaves for garnish
- Olive oil for frying

Directions

1. In one bowl, beat eggs, and in another bowl, combine breadcrumbs and grated Parmesan.
2. Dip eggplant slices in egg, then coat with breadcrumb mixture.
3. Heat olive oil in a pan and fry eggplant slices until golden.
4. In a baking dish, layer fried eggplant, marinara sauce, and mozzarella cheese.
5. Bake in a preheated oven at 375°F (190°C) until the cheese is bubbly and golden.
6. Garnish with fresh basil leaves.

Fun Facts

Eggplant Parmesan is a beloved Italian dish, often enjoyed for its crispy texture and cheesy goodness.

4 servings   360 cal   35 min

Spinach and Ricotta Stuffed Shells

Jumbo pasta shells filled with a creamy spinach and ricotta cheese mixture, baked in marinara sauce.

Ingredients:

- 16 jumbo pasta shells
- 2 cups ricotta cheese
- 1 cup chopped spinach, cooked and drained
- 1 cup shredded mozzarella cheese
- 1/2 cup grated Parmesan cheese
- 2 cups marinara sauce
- Fresh basil leaves for garnish

Directions

1. Cook pasta shells according to package instructions, then drain.
2. In a bowl, mix ricotta cheese, chopped spinach, mozzarella cheese, and grated Parmesan.
3. Stuff each pasta shell with the ricotta mixture.
4. Spread marinara sauce in a baking dish and place stuffed shells on top.
5. Bake in a preheated oven at 350°F (175°C) until heated through and bubbly.
6. Garnish with fresh basil leaves.

Fun Facts

Stuffed shells are a classic Italian comfort food, known for their cheesy and flavorful filling.

4 servings 420 cal 45 min

Moroccan Tagine with Poached Eggs

A Moroccan tagine featuring a flavorful tomato-based sauce with poached eggs and spices.

Ingredients:

- 4 large eggs
- 2 onions, chopped
- 2 cloves garlic, minced
- 1 can of diced tomatoes
- 1/2 cup vegetable broth
- Ground cumin, paprika, and cayenne pepper for seasoning
- Fresh cilantro for garnish
- Olive oil for cooking

Directions

1. In a tagine or a large skillet, sauté onions and garlic in olive oil until softened.
2. Add diced tomatoes, vegetable broth, and spices. Simmer until the sauce thickens.
3. Create small wells in the sauce and poach eggs in them until the whites are set but the yolks are still runny.
4. Serve hot, garnished with fresh cilantro.

Fun Facts

Tagines are traditional Moroccan stews, often cooked in a cone-shaped clay pot that retains moisture and flavor.

4 servings — 450 cal — 50 min

Spanish Seafood Paella

A classic Spanish paella with a flavorful mix of seafood, saffron-infused rice, and perfectly poached eggs.

Ingredients:

- 2 cups Arborio rice
- 4 cups chicken broth
- 8 large shrimp
- 8 mussels
- 8 clams
- 1/2 cup diced bell pepper
- 1/2 cup frozen peas
- 1/4 tsp saffron threads
- Olive oil for cooking
- Fresh parsley and lemon wedges for garnish

Directions

1. In a paella pan or large skillet, heat olive oil and sauté diced bell pepper until tender.
2. Add Arborio rice and saffron threads, stirring to coat with the oil.
3. Pour in chicken broth and simmer until the rice is almost cooked.
4. Arrange seafood, clams, mussels, and shrimp on top of the rice.
5. Cover and cook until the seafood is cooked and the rice is tender.
6. Create small wells and poach eggs until the whites are set but the yolks are still runny.
7. Garnish with fresh parsley and lemon wedges.

Fun Facts

Paella is a famous Spanish dish known for its vibrant colors and rich, saffron-infused flavor.

4 servings | 360 cal | 30 min

Egg Fried Rice with Shrimp

Normal

A delicious Chinese fried rice with plump shrimp, scrambled eggs, and an array of vegetables.

Ingredients:

- 2 cups cooked and cooled rice
- 12 large shrimp, peeled and deveined
- 4 large eggs
- Assorted vegetables (e.g., peas, carrots, bell peppers)
- Soy sauce and sesame oil for seasoning
- Green onions for garnish

Directions

1. Heat a wok or a large pan with oil and stir-fry shrimp until pink and opaque. Remove from the pan.
2. Scramble eggs in the same pan until cooked, then set aside.
3. Stir-fry assorted vegetables until tender, then add rice and cooked shrimp back to the pan.
4. Drizzle with soy sauce and sesame oil and stir in scrambled eggs.
5. Garnish with chopped green onions.

Fun Facts

Egg fried rice is a popular Chinese dish, known for its savory and flavorful combination of ingredients.

Chapter 7:
Egg Sides and Accompaniments

4 servings | 320 cal | 30 min

Garlic Parmesan Eggplant Fries

Crispy eggplant fries coated in garlic and Parmesan, perfect for dipping.

Ingredients:

- 2 large eggplants, cut into fries
- 2 large eggs
- 1 cup breadcrumbs
- 1/2 cup grated Parmesan cheese
- 2 cloves garlic, minced
- Salt and pepper, to taste
- Olive oil for frying

Directions

1. In one bowl, beat eggs, and in another bowl, combine breadcrumbs, grated Parmesan, minced garlic, salt, and pepper.
2. Dip eggplant fries in egg, then coat with the breadcrumb mixture.
3. Heat olive oil in a pan and fry eggplant fries until golden and crispy.
4. Drain on paper towels and serve hot.

Fun Facts

Eggplant fries make for a delightful and crunchy side dish, perfect for dipping in your favorite sauce.

4 servings   280 cal   25 min

Creamed Spinach with Poached Eggs

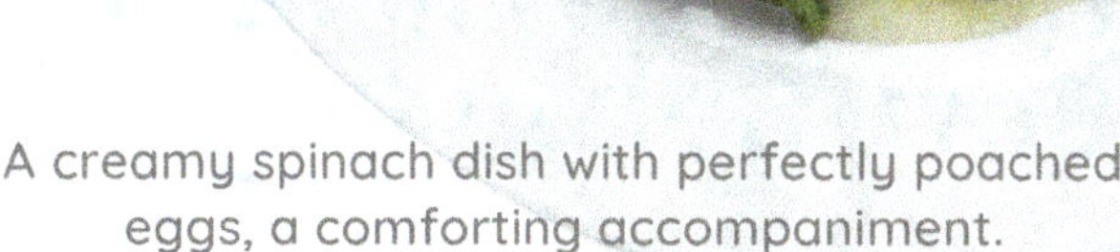

A creamy spinach dish with perfectly poached eggs, a comforting accompaniment.

Ingredients:

- 4 large eggs
- 8 cups fresh spinach
- 1 cup heavy cream
- 2 cloves garlic, minced
- Grated nutmeg and cayenne pepper, to taste
- Butter for sautéing

Directions

1. Sauté minced garlic in butter until fragrant, then add fresh spinach and cook until wilted.
2. In a separate pot, heat heavy cream and season with grated nutmeg and cayenne pepper.
3. Poach eggs until the whites are set but the yolks are still runny.
4. Serve poached eggs over the creamy spinach.

Fun Facts

Creamed spinach is a classic side dish known for its smooth texture and rich, savory flavor.

4 servings 320 cal 30 min

Baked Beans with Soft-Boiled Eggs

Hearty baked beans with soft-boiled eggs, a comforting dish with a touch of nostalgia.

Ingredients:

- 4 large eggs
- 2 cans of baked beans
- 1/4 cup brown sugar
- 2 tbsp molasses
- 1/2 cup diced onion
- 4 slices of bacon
- Salt and pepper, to taste

Directions

1. In a saucepan, cook bacon until crispy, then remove and crumble it.
2. In the same pan, sauté diced onion until tender.
3. Add baked beans, brown sugar, and molasses. Simmer until heated through.
4. Soft-boil eggs and serve them on top of the baked beans.
5. Garnish with crumbled bacon.

Fun Facts

Baked beans and eggs are a classic comfort food combination often enjoyed for breakfast or brunch.

4 servings   280 cal   25 min

Roasted Brussels Sprouts with Fried Egg

Roasted Brussels sprouts with a crispy fried egg, a flavorful and hearty side.

Ingredients:

- 1 lb Brussels sprouts, trimmed and halved
- 4 large eggs
- Olive oil
- Salt and pepper, to taste
- Grated Parmesan cheese for garnish
- Balsamic glaze for drizzling

Directions

1. Toss Brussels sprouts in olive oil, salt, and pepper, then roast in a preheated oven at 400°F (200°C) until tender and crispy.
2. Fry eggs sunny side up in a separate pan.
3. Serve fried eggs on top of roasted Brussels sprouts.
4. Garnish with grated Parmesan cheese and a drizzle of balsamic glaze.

Fun Facts

Brussels sprouts are known for their nutty flavor, and roasting enhances their crispiness and taste.

4 servings

320 cal

30 min

Polenta Fries with Dipping Sauce

Crispy polenta fries served with a flavorful dipping sauce, a delightful side dish.

Ingredients:

- 1 cup instant polenta
- 4 cups water
- 1/2 cup grated Parmesan cheese
- Salt and pepper, to taste
- Olive oil for frying
- Dipping sauce (e.g., marinara, aioli, or pesto)

Directions

1. Cook polenta by boiling water and whisking in the polenta until it thickens.
2. Stir in grated Parmesan, salt, and pepper.
3. Pour the polenta into a greased dish and refrigerate until firm.
4. Cut polenta into fries and fry them until golden and crispy.
5. Serve with your favorite dipping sauce.

Fun Facts

Polenta fries are a satisfying and versatile side dish, perfect for dipping in a variety of sauces.

4 servings | 280 cal | 30 min

Mashed Cauliflower with Scrambled Eggs

Creamy mashed cauliflower served with a side of fluffy scrambled eggs.

Ingredients:

- 1 large head of cauliflower, cut into florets
- 4 large eggs
- 1/2 cup heavy cream
- Butter
- Salt and pepper, to taste
- Chopped chives for garnish

Directions

1. Steam cauliflower florets until tender, then mash with a potato masher or blender.
2. In a pan, scramble eggs in butter until cooked to your liking.
3. Mix heavy cream into the mashed cauliflower until creamy and smooth.
4. Season with salt and pepper.
5. Serve with scrambled eggs on the side and garnish with chopped chives.

Fun Facts

Mashed cauliflower is a low-carb alternative to mashed potatoes, known for its creamy texture and neutral flavor.

4 servings | 320 cal | 25 min

Egg and Vegetable Fried Rice

A flavorful fried rice with assorted vegetables and scrambled eggs.

Ingredients:

- 2 cups cooked and cooled rice
- 4 large eggs
- Assorted vegetables (e.g., peas, carrots, bell peppers)
- Soy sauce and sesame oil for seasoning
- Green onions for garnish

Directions

1. Heat a wok or a large pan with oil and stir-fry assorted vegetables until tender.
2. Push the vegetables to one side and scramble eggs on the other side until cooked.
3. Mix in cooked rice and season with soy sauce and sesame oil.
4. Garnish with chopped green onions.

Fun Facts

Egg and vegetable fried rice is a classic Asian dish known for its savory and satisfying flavors.

4 servings   340 cal   30 min

Cheesy Grits with Sunny-Side-Up Eggs

Easy

Creamy and cheesy grits topped with perfectly cooked sunny-side-up eggs.

Ingredients:

- 1 cup grits
- 4 cups water
- 1 cup grated cheddar cheese
- 4 large eggs
- Butter
- Salt and pepper, to taste
- Hot sauce for drizzling

Directions

1. Cook grits by boiling water and stirring in the grits until they thicken.
2. Stir in grated cheddar cheese, butter, salt, and pepper until creamy.
3. Fry eggs sunny side up in a separate pan.
4. Serve sunny-side-up eggs on top of the cheesy grits.
5. Drizzle with hot sauce.

Fun Facts

Cheesy grits are a popular Southern dish, known for their rich and comforting texture, often served for breakfast or as a side dish.

4 servings   340 cal   40 min

A delightful combination of breaded and fried eggplant and zucchini slices with tomato sauce and melted cheese.

Eggplant and Zucchini Parmesan

Ingredients:

- 2 large eggplants, sliced
- 2 large zucchinis, sliced
- 4 large eggs
- 1 cup breadcrumbs
- 1 cup grated Parmesan cheese
- 2 cups marinara sauce
- 2 cups shredded mozzarella cheese
- Fresh basil leaves for garnish
- Olive oil for frying

Directions

1. In one bowl, beat eggs, and in another bowl, combine breadcrumbs and grated Parmesan.
2. Dip eggplant and zucchini slices in egg, then coat with the breadcrumb mixture.
3. Heat olive oil in a pan and fry slices until golden and crispy.
4. In a baking dish, layer fried eggplant and zucchini, marinara sauce, and mozzarella cheese.
5. Bake in a preheated oven at 375°F (190°C) until the cheese is bubbly and golden.
6. Garnish with fresh basil leaves.

Fun Facts

Eggplant and zucchini Parmesan is a delicious Italian dish, often enjoyed for its crispy texture and cheesy goodness.

4 servings | 360 cal | 35 min

Savory Bread Pudding with Eggs

A savory bread pudding with eggs, cheese, and your favorite herbs and spices.

Ingredients:

- 4 large eggs
- 4 cups stale bread, cubed
- 1 cup milk
- 1 cup shredded cheddar cheese
- Chopped herbs (e.g., thyme, rosemary, or chives)
- Salt and pepper, to taste

Directions

1. Whisk eggs, milk, and chopped herbs together, then season with salt and pepper.
2. In a baking dish, layer stale bread cubes and shredded cheddar cheese.
3. Pour the egg mixture over the bread and cheese.
4. Bake in a preheated oven at 350°F (175°C) until the top is golden and the pudding is set.

Fun Facts

Savory bread pudding is a versatile dish, perfect for using up stale bread and customizing with your favorite ingredients.

Chapter 8:
Egg Soups and Broths

4 servings | 280 cal | 30 min

Italian Stracciatella Soup

A comforting Italian egg drop soup with spinach and Parmesan.

Ingredients:

- 4 cups chicken broth
- 4 large eggs
- 1/2 cup grated Parmesan cheese
- 2 cups fresh spinach
- Salt and pepper, to taste

Directions

1. In a pot, bring chicken broth to a simmer.
2. Beat eggs and Parmesan cheese together.
3. Slowly pour the egg mixture into the simmering broth, stirring to create ribbons of egg.
4. Add fresh spinach and cook until wilted.
5. Season with salt and pepper, and serve hot.

Fun Facts

Stracciatella means "little shreds" in Italian, referring to the delicate egg ribbons in the soup.

4 servings   320 cal   30 min

Avgolemono Greek Soup

A traditional Greek soup with a creamy lemon and egg broth.

Ingredients:

- 4 cups chicken broth
- 1/2 cup orzo pasta
- 4 large eggs
- Juice of 2 lemons
- Salt and pepper, to taste
- Chopped fresh dill for garnish

Directions

1. In a pot, bring chicken broth to a boil and add orzo pasta. Cook until tender.
2. In a bowl, beat eggs and lemon juice until frothy.
3. Slowly add a ladle of hot broth to the egg mixture, whisking constantly.
4. Pour the egg mixture back into the pot, stirring constantly until the soup thickens.
5. Season with salt and pepper, and garnish with fresh dill.

Fun Facts

Avgolemono soup is a classic Greek dish, known for its silky and tangy broth.

4 servings | 380 cal | 45 min

Vietnamese Pho with Poached Egg

Normal

A fragrant Vietnamese noodle soup with poached eggs and tender beef.

Ingredients:

- 4 large eggs
- 8 cups beef broth
- 8 oz rice noodles
- 8 oz beef slices
- Fresh herbs (e.g., cilantro, mint, and Thai basil)
- Bean sprouts, lime wedges, and hoisin sauce for garnish

Directions

1. Soft-boil eggs, cool, and peel them.
2. Cook rice noodles according to package instructions, then drain.
3. In a pot, heat beef broth and add beef slices to cook until tender.
4. Divide cooked rice noodles, beef, and herbs among bowls.
5. Top with a soft-boiled egg and serve with bean sprouts, lime wedges, and hoisin sauce.

Fun Facts

Pho is a beloved Vietnamese soup, known for its aromatic broth and fresh ingredients.

4 servings   340 cal   35 min

Mexican Tortilla Soup with Egg

A flavorful Mexican tortilla soup with crispy tortilla strips and a poached egg.

Ingredients:

- 4 large eggs
- 4 corn tortillas, sliced into strips
- 8 cups chicken broth
- 1 can diced tomatoes
- 1 onion, chopped
- 2 cloves garlic, minced
- Ground cumin and chili powder, to taste

Directions

1. In a pan, heat a bit of oil and fry corn tortilla strips until crispy.
2. In a pot, sauté chopped onion and minced garlic until tender.
3. Add diced tomatoes, chicken broth, ground cumin, and chili powder. Simmer until flavors meld.
4. Poach eggs in the simmering soup until the whites are set but the yolks are still runny.
5. Serve hot, garnished with crispy tortilla strips.

Fun Facts

Tortilla soup is a classic Mexican dish, known for its rich, spicy broth and crunchy tortilla strips.

4 servings   340 cal   40 min

Russian Borscht with Hard-Boiled Eggs

A hearty Russian borscht with beets, cabbage, and slices of hard-boiled eggs.

Ingredients:

- 4 large eggs
- 2 large beets, peeled and grated
- 4 cups beef broth
- 1/2 head cabbage, shredded
- 1 onion, chopped
- 2 cloves garlic, minced
- Sour cream and fresh dill for garnish

Directions

1. Hard-boil eggs, cool, peel, and slice them.
2. In a pot, combine grated beets and beef broth. Simmer until beets are tender.
3. Add shredded cabbage, chopped onion, and minced garlic. Simmer until cabbage is tender.
4. Season with salt and pepper.
5. Serve hot, garnished with slices of hard-boiled eggs, sour cream, and fresh dill.

Fun Facts

Borscht is a traditional Russian soup, known for its vibrant color and earthy flavor, often served with sour cream.

4 servings | 300 cal | 35 min

Chinese Hot and Sour Egg Drop Soup

A Chinese soup with a balance of hot and sour flavors, featuring egg ribbons.

Ingredients:

- 4 large eggs
- 8 cups chicken broth
- 4 oz tofu, cubed
- 2 tbsp soy sauce
- 1 tbsp rice vinegar
- 1 tsp chili sauce
- Cornstarch slurry (for thickening)
- Sliced green onions for garnish

Directions

1. In a pot, bring chicken broth to a simmer.
2. Add tofu, soy sauce, rice vinegar, and chili sauce. Simmer until tofu is heated through.
3. Create egg ribbons by slowly pouring beaten eggs into the simmering broth, stirring gently.
4. Thicken the soup with cornstarch slurry to your desired consistency.
5. Garnish with sliced green onions.

Fun Facts

Hot and sour soup is a popular Chinese dish known for its contrasting flavors and silky egg ribbons.

4 servings   280 cal   25 min

Spanish Garlic Soup with Poached Egg

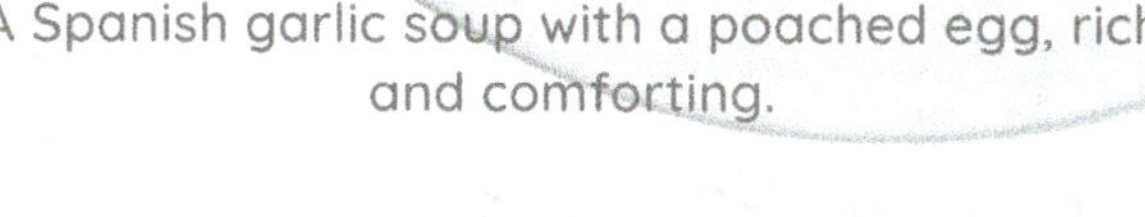

A Spanish garlic soup with a poached egg, rich and comforting.

Ingredients:

- 4 large eggs
- 8 cups chicken broth
- 4 slices of rustic bread
- 6 cloves garlic, minced
- Smoked paprika and olive oil for seasoning
- Chopped fresh parsley for garnish

Directions

1. In a pot, heat olive oil and sauté minced garlic until fragrant.
2. Sprinkle with smoked paprika and add slices of rustic bread to toast.
3. Pour in chicken broth and simmer until the bread absorbs the flavors.
4. Poach eggs in the simmering soup until the whites are set but the yolks are still runny.
5. Garnish with chopped fresh parsley.

Fun Facts

Spanish garlic soup, also known as "Sopa de Ajo," is a traditional Castilian dish, known for its simple yet flavorful ingredients.

4 servings | 320 cal | 35 min

A spicy and sour Thai Tom Yum soup with the addition of poached eggs.

Thai Tom Yum Soup with Poached Egg

Ingredients:

- 4 large eggs
- 8 cups chicken broth
- 4 oz shrimp
- 4 oz mushrooms
- Lemongrass, galangal, lime leaves, and Thai chili for seasoning
- Lime wedges and cilantro for garnish

Directions

1. In a pot, bring chicken broth to a boil and add lemongrass, galangal, lime leaves, and Thai chili. Simmer to infuse the flavors.
2. Add shrimp and mushrooms to the simmering soup and cook until shrimp turn pink.
3. Poach eggs in the soup until the whites are set but the yolks are still runny.
4. Serve with lime wedges and fresh cilantro.

Fun Facts

Tom Yum soup is a popular Thai dish known for its bold and vibrant flavors, combining spicy and sour elements.

4 servings   360 cal   40 min

Indian Mulligatawny Soup

Normal

A hearty Indian soup with lentils, vegetables, and a touch of poached egg.

Ingredients:

- 4 large eggs
- 1 cup red lentils
- 8 cups chicken broth
- 1 onion, chopped
- 2 carrots, diced
- 2 cloves garlic, minced
- Ground turmeric and curry powder for seasoning
- Chopped fresh cilantro for garnish

Directions

1. In a pot, heat a bit of oil and sauté chopped onion and minced garlic until tender.
2. Add diced carrots, red lentils, and chicken broth. Simmer until lentils are soft.
3. Season with ground turmeric and curry powder.
4. Poach eggs in the simmering soup until the whites are set but the yolks are still runny.
5. Garnish with chopped fresh cilantro.

Fun Facts

Mulligatawny soup is a flavorful Indian dish, known for its rich and aromatic spices.

4 servings   320 cal   35 min

Creamy Tomato Bisque with Poached Egg

A creamy tomato bisque with the added richness of a poached egg.

Ingredients:

- 4 large eggs
- 4 cups tomato soup
- 1/2 cup heavy cream
- Basil leaves for garnish
- Salt and pepper, to taste

Directions

1. Heat tomato soup in a pot and stir in heavy cream.
2. Season with salt and pepper to taste.
3. Poach eggs in the simmering soup until the whites are set but the yolks are still runny.
4. Serve hot, garnished with basil leaves.

Fun Facts

Tomato bisque is a classic creamy tomato soup, known for its smooth and velvety texture.

Chapter 9:
Egg Salads and Bowls

4 servings   380 cal   30 min

Cobb Salad with Poached Egg

Easy

A classic Cobb salad with a perfectly poached egg, a delightful meal in a bowl.

Ingredients:

- 4 large eggs
- 2 cups mixed greens
- 2 cups cooked chicken, diced
- 8 strips of bacon, cooked and crumbled
- 2 ripe avocados, diced
- 1 cup cherry tomatoes, halved
- 1/2 cup blue cheese, crumbled
- 1/2 cup red wine vinaigrette
- Salt and pepper, to taste

Directions

1. Soft-boil eggs, cool, peel, and slice them.
2. In a large bowl, arrange mixed greens and top with diced chicken, bacon, avocado, cherry tomatoes, and blue cheese.
3. Drizzle with red wine vinaigrette and season with salt and pepper.
4. Place soft-boiled eggs on top and serve.

Fun Facts

The Cobb salad is a classic American dish, known for its combination of fresh ingredients and flavors.

4 servings 320 cal 25 min

Quinoa and Egg Breakfast Bowl

Easy

A nutritious breakfast bowl with quinoa, poached eggs, and an array of toppings.

Ingredients:

- 4 large eggs
- 2 cups cooked quinoa
- Sliced fresh fruit (e.g., berries, banana, or kiwi)
- Nuts and seeds (e.g., almonds, chia seeds, or sunflower seeds)
- Greek yogurt
- Honey or maple syrup for drizzling

Directions

1. Poach eggs to your desired level of doneness.
2. Divide cooked quinoa among bowls and top with sliced fresh fruit, nuts, seeds, and Greek yogurt.
3. Place a poached egg on top of each bowl.
4. Drizzle with honey or maple syrup for sweetness.

Fun Facts

Breakfast bowls are a trendy and customizable way to start your day with a healthy and satisfying meal.

4 servings | 360 cal | 30 min

Mediterranean Chickpea Salad with Egg

A Mediterranean-inspired chickpea salad with hard-boiled eggs and fresh herbs.

Ingredients:

- 4 large eggs
- 2 cans of chickpeas, drained and rinsed
- 1 cup cherry tomatoes, halved
- 1 cucumber, diced
- 1/2 red onion, finely chopped
- Fresh parsley and mint leaves
- Feta cheese for garnish
- Lemon vinaigrette
- Olive oil, salt, and pepper for seasoning

Directions

1. Hard-boil eggs, cool, peel, and quarter them.
2. In a large bowl, combine chickpeas, cherry tomatoes, cucumber, and red onion.
3. Add fresh parsley and mint leaves.
4. Drizzle with lemon vinaigrette and season with olive oil, salt, and pepper.
5. Top with quartered hard-boiled eggs and crumbled feta cheese.

Fun Facts

Mediterranean chickpea salad is a refreshing and vibrant dish, known for its mix of textures and flavors.

4 servings   400 cal   35 min

Chicken and Egg Caesar Salad

A classic Caesar salad with grilled chicken, hard-boiled eggs, and creamy dressing.

Ingredients:

- 4 large eggs
- 2 boneless, skinless chicken breasts
- 8 cups Romaine lettuce, torn into bite-sized pieces
- 1 cup croutons
- Grated Parmesan cheese for garnish
- Caesar dressing
- Olive oil, salt, and pepper for seasoning

Directions

1. Hard-boil eggs, cool, peel, and slice them.
2. Season chicken breasts with olive oil, salt, and pepper, then grill until cooked through.
3. In a large bowl, combine torn Romaine lettuce, croutons, and grated Parmesan cheese.
4. Drizzle with Caesar dressing and toss to coat.
5. Top with sliced hard-boiled eggs and grilled chicken.

Fun Facts

Caesar salad is a beloved classic, known for its rich and creamy dressing and crisp Romaine lettuce.

4 servings

320 cal

25 min

Tuna and Egg Salad

Easy

A protein-packed tuna and egg salad with a creamy dressing.

Ingredients:

- 4 large eggs
- 2 cans of tuna, drained
- 1/2 cup mayonnaise
- 1/4 cup chopped celery
- 1/4 cup diced red onion
- Dill pickles, chopped
- Dijon mustard, lemon juice, and salt and pepper for seasoning

Directions

1. Hard-boil eggs, cool, peel, and chop them.
2. In a bowl, combine chopped eggs, drained tuna, mayonnaise, chopped celery, diced red onion, and dill pickles.
3. Season with Dijon mustard, lemon juice, salt, and pepper.
4. Mix until well combined and serve.

Fun Facts

Tuna and egg salad is a classic combination, known for its creamy and savory flavors.

4 servings | 340 cal | 30 min

Egg and Avocado Breakfast Bowl

A wholesome breakfast bowl with eggs, avocado, and a variety of toppings.

Ingredients:

- 4 large eggs
- 2 ripe avocados, halved and pitted
- Sliced fresh fruit (e.g., strawberries, kiwi, or mango)
- Granola and yogurt
- Honey or maple syrup for drizzling

Directions

1. Poach eggs to your desired level of doneness.
2. Scoop out some flesh from each avocado half to create a well.
3. Fill the avocado halves with poached eggs and top with sliced fresh fruit and granola.
4. Serve with a dollop of yogurt and a drizzle of honey or maple syrup.

Fun Facts

Breakfast bowls with avocado are a popular and nutritious way to start your day with a filling meal.

4 servings   340 cal   30 min

Greek Salad with Poached Egg

A traditional Greek salad with a poached egg, bringing a new twist to a classic.

Ingredients:

- 4 large eggs
- 2 cups cherry tomatoes, halved
- 1 cucumber, diced
- 1/2 red onion, thinly sliced
- Kalamata olives
- Feta cheese for garnish
- Greek dressing
- Olive oil, salt, and pepper for seasoning

Directions

1. Poach eggs to your desired level of doneness.
2. In a bowl, combine cherry tomatoes, cucumber, red onion, Kalamata olives, and feta cheese.
3. Drizzle with Greek dressing and season with olive oil, salt, and pepper.
4. Place a poached egg on top of each salad and serve.

Fun Facts

Adding a poached egg to a Greek salad gives it an extra creamy and rich dimension.

4 servings   360 cal   35 min

Mexican Chopped Salad with Egg

Normal

A colorful Mexican chopped salad with hard-boiled eggs and zesty flavors.

Ingredients:

- 4 large eggs
- 2 cups Romaine lettuce, chopped
- 1 cup corn kernels
- 1 cup black beans, drained and rinsed
- 1 red bell pepper, diced
- 1 avocado, diced
- Cherry tomatoes, halved
- Cilantro and lime wedges for garnish
- Mexican-inspired dressing
- Olive oil, salt, and pepper for seasoning

Directions

1. Hard-boil eggs, cool, peel, and slice them.
2. In a large bowl, combine chopped Romaine lettuce, corn kernels, black beans, diced red bell pepper, avocado, and cherry tomatoes.
3. Drizzle with Mexican-inspired dressing and season with olive oil, salt, and pepper.
4. Top with sliced hard-boiled eggs, cilantro, and lime wedges.

Fun Facts

Mexican chopped salad is a vibrant and flavorful dish, known for its zesty and zingy taste.

4 servings   340 cal   25 min

Caprese Egg Salad

A Caprese-inspired egg salad with fresh mozzarella, basil, and a balsamic glaze.

Ingredients:

- 4 large eggs
- 2 cups cherry tomatoes, halved
- Fresh mozzarella balls
- Fresh basil leaves
- Balsamic glaze
- Olive oil, salt, and pepper for seasoning

Directions

1. Hard-boil eggs, cool, peel, and slice them.
2. In a bowl, combine cherry tomatoes, fresh mozzarella balls, and fresh basil leaves.
3. Drizzle with balsamic glaze and season with olive oil, salt, and pepper.
4. Top with sliced hard-boiled eggs.

Fun Facts

The Caprese egg salad is a delightful twist on the classic Caprese salad, combining fresh ingredients with boiled eggs.

4 servings   380 cal   30 min

Asian Noodle Salad with Poached Egg

An Asian-inspired noodle salad with a perfectly poached egg on top.

Ingredients:

- 4 large eggs
- 8 oz Asian noodles
- 1 cup mixed vegetables (e.g., bell peppers, carrots, and cucumber)
- Chopped scallions and cilantro for garnish
- Sesame dressing
- Soy sauce, sesame oil, and rice vinegar for seasoning

Directions

1. Poach eggs to your desired level of doneness.
2. Cook Asian noodles according to package instructions, then rinse with cold water.
3. Toss noodles with mixed vegetables and drizzle with sesame dressing.
4. Season with soy sauce, sesame oil, and rice vinegar to taste.
5. Place a poached egg on top and garnish with chopped scallions and cilantro.

Fun Facts

Asian noodle salads are known for their delightful combination of flavors and textures, with a poached egg adding a creamy element.

Chapter 10:
Egg Desserts and Sweets

4 servings 350 cal 40 min

Chocolate Mousse with Egg Whites

A silky chocolate mousse made with fluffy egg whites.

Ingredients:

- 4 large egg whites
- 8 oz semisweet chocolate, melted
- 1/4 cup sugar
- 1 tsp vanilla extract
- Pinch of salt
- Whipped cream and chocolate shavings for garnish

Directions

1. In a bowl, beat egg whites until stiff peaks form.
2. In another bowl, combine melted chocolate, sugar, vanilla extract, and a pinch of salt.
3. Gently fold the egg whites into the chocolate mixture until well combined.
4. Divide the mousse into serving dishes and refrigerate until set.
5. Garnish with whipped cream and chocolate shavings.

Fun Facts

Chocolate mousse is a classic dessert, known for its airy and creamy texture, a true delight for chocolate lovers.

4 servings — 320 cal — 45 min

Lemon Curd Tart with Meringue

A zesty lemon curd tart topped with a fluffy meringue.

Ingredients:

- 4 large eggs
- 1 cup sugar
- Zest and juice of 2 lemons
- 1/2 cup butter
- 1 pre-baked tart shell
- 4 large egg whites
- 1/2 cup sugar

Directions

1. In a saucepan, whisk together eggs, sugar, lemon zest, and lemon juice.
2. Cook over low heat, stirring, until the mixture thickens.
3. Remove from heat and stir in butter until melted.
4. Pour the lemon curd into the pre-baked tart shell.
5. In a bowl, beat egg whites until soft peaks form, then gradually add sugar to make a meringue.
6. Spread the meringue over the lemon curd and bake until the top is golden.
7. Cool before serving.

Fun Facts

Lemon curd tart with meringue is a tangy and sweet dessert, known for its contrast of flavors and textures.

4 servings | 320 cal | 40 min

Crème Brûlée

A classic Crème Brûlée with a perfectly caramelized sugar crust.

Ingredients:

- 4 large egg yolks
- 1/2 cup sugar
- 2 cups heavy cream
- 1 tsp vanilla extract
- Brown sugar for caramelizing

Directions

1. Preheat the oven to 325°F (160°C).
2. In a bowl, whisk together egg yolks and sugar until well combined.
3. Heat heavy cream until it's hot but not boiling, then stir in vanilla extract.
4. Gradually whisk the cream into the egg yolk mixture.
5. Strain the mixture and pour it into ramekins.
6. Place ramekins in a water bath and bake until set.
7. Chill in the refrigerator until cold.
8. Sprinkle brown sugar on top and caramelize with a torch.

Fun Facts

Crème Brûlée is a classic French dessert, known for its rich custard and crackling caramelized sugar top.

4 servings | 360 cal | 45 min

Tiramisu with Ladyfingers

A traditional Tiramisu with ladyfingers soaked in espresso and layered with mascarpone.

Ingredients:

- 4 large eggs
- 1 cup mascarpone cheese
- 1/2 cup sugar
- 1 cup brewed espresso, cooled
- Ladyfingers
- Cocoa powder for dusting

Directions

1. In a bowl, beat egg yolks and sugar until creamy and pale.
2. Mix in mascarpone cheese until smooth.
3. In another bowl, beat egg whites until stiff peaks form, then fold into the mascarpone mixture.
4. Quickly dip ladyfingers in brewed espresso and layer them in serving glasses.
5. Spread the mascarpone mixture over the ladyfingers.
6. Repeat the layers and finish with a dusting of cocoa powder.
7. Chill before serving.

Fun Facts

Tiramisu is a beloved Italian dessert, known for its layers of coffee-soaked ladyfingers and creamy mascarpone.

4 servings

340 cal

35 min

Panna Cotta with Berry Compote

A creamy panna cotta topped with a sweet and tangy berry compote.

Ingredients:

- 4 cups heavy cream
- 1/2 cup sugar
- 2 tsp vanilla extract
- 2 tsp gelatin powder
- Mixed berries (e.g., strawberries, blueberries, and raspberries)
- Sugar and lemon juice for the compote

Directions

1. In a saucepan, heat heavy cream and sugar, stirring until sugar is dissolved.
2. Stir in vanilla extract and gelatin powder until fully dissolved.
3. Pour the mixture into serving glasses and chill until set.
4. In a separate saucepan, cook mixed berries with sugar and lemon juice until the berries break down.
5. Serve the panna cotta topped with the berry compote.

Fun Facts

Panna cotta is an Italian dessert, known for its creamy texture and versatility in pairing with various toppings.

4 servings | 380 cal | 50 min

Coconut Custard Pie

A delightful coconut custard pie with a flaky crust.

Ingredients:

- 4 large eggs
- 1 cup sugar
- 1/2 cup butter, melted
- 1 cup shredded coconut
- 1 tsp vanilla extract
- 1 pie crust

Directions

1. Preheat the oven to 350°F (175°C).
2. In a bowl, whisk together eggs, sugar, melted butter, shredded coconut, and vanilla extract.
3. Pour the mixture into the pie crust.
4. Bake until the top is golden and the custard is set.
5. Cool before serving.

Fun Facts

Coconut custard pie is a classic dessert, known for its sweet and creamy filling and flaky pastry.

4 servings 360 cal 30 min

Eggless Brownies

A delicious batch of eggless brownies that are moist and fudgy.

Ingredients:

- 1/2 cup butter, melted
- 1 cup sugar
- 1/4 cup unsweetened cocoa powder
- 1/2 cup all-purpose flour
- 1/4 tsp salt
- 1/4 tsp baking powder
- 1 tsp vanilla extract
- Chopped nuts or chocolate chips (optional)

Directions

1. Preheat the oven to 350°F (175°C).
2. In a bowl, mix melted butter and sugar until well combined.
3. Stir in cocoa powder, flour, salt, baking powder, and vanilla extract.
4. Add chopped nuts or chocolate chips if desired.
5. Spread the batter in a greased baking pan.
6. Bake until a toothpick comes out with moist crumbs.
7. Cool before cutting into squares.

Fun Facts

Eggless brownies are a delightful treat, perfect for those with egg allergies or as a vegan option.

4 servings | 400 cal | 50 min

Light and airy éclairs filled with luscious vanilla custard.

Custard-Filled Eclairs

Ingredients:

- 4 large eggs
- 1/2 cup unsalted butter
- 1 cup water
- 1 cup all-purpose flour
- 1/4 tsp salt
- 2 cups milk
- 1/2 cup sugar
- 2 tsp vanilla extract
- Powdered sugar for dusting

Fun Facts

Custard-filled éclairs are a delightful pastry, known for their airy choux pastry and creamy custard filling.

Directions

1. Preheat the oven to 375°F (190°C).
2. In a saucepan, melt butter in water, then stir in flour and salt until a smooth dough forms.
3. Remove from heat and stir in eggs one at a time until well combined.
4. Pipe or spoon the dough onto a baking sheet, forming éclair shapes.
5. Bake until golden and puffed.
6. In another saucepan, heat milk, sugar, and vanilla extract until hot but not boiling.
7. Whisk a bit of the hot milk mixture into the remaining eggs, then return it to the saucepan and cook until it thickens into custard.
8. Slice éclairs in half and fill with custard.
9. Dust with powdered sugar before serving.

4 servings   360 cal   35 min

Normal

Mocha Pots de Crème

A velvety mocha pots de crème, combining coffee and chocolate flavors.

Ingredients:

- 4 large eggs
- 1/2 cup sugar
- 1/4 cup unsweetened cocoa powder
- 1/4 cup espresso or strong coffee
- 1 cup heavy cream
- 1 tsp vanilla extract

Directions

1. Preheat the oven to 325°F (160°C).
2. In a bowl, whisk together eggs and sugar until smooth and creamy.
3. Mix in cocoa powder, espresso, heavy cream, and vanilla extract until well combined.
4. Pour the mixture into ramekins and place them in a water bath.
5. Bake until set.
6. Chill before serving.

Fun Facts

Pots de crème are a French dessert, known for their silky and rich custard-like texture.

4 servings   340 cal   45 min

Strawberry Shortcake with Whipped Egg Cream

A classic strawberry shortcake with a delightful whipped egg cream.

Ingredients:

- 4 large eggs
- 1 cup sugar
- 2 cups sliced strawberries
- 2 cups whipped cream
- 1 tsp vanilla extract
- Shortcakes for serving

Directions

1. Preheat the oven to 350°F (175°C).
2. In a bowl, beat eggs and sugar until fluffy and pale.
3. Mix in sliced strawberries and set aside to macerate.
4. In another bowl, whip egg cream and vanilla extract until stiff peaks form.
5. Slice shortcakes and spoon strawberry mixture on top.
6. Dollop with whipped egg cream and serve.

Fun Facts

Strawberry shortcake is a beloved dessert, known for its sweet and fruity layers of goodness.

We have a small favor to ask

As we savor the last bites of our journey through the "Best of Eggs Cookbook: Crack & Cook - Master the Best Egg Dishes with 100+ Delectable Creations," I want to share a humble plea.

Reviews, my fellow egg enthusiasts, are like the perfectly poached egg—delicate, essential, and immensely satisfying. For a small publisher like us, they are the golden yolks that nourish our creative endeavors.

If you could spare a moment, kindly revisit the platform where you discovered this eggstravaganza—whether it's an app or an online marketplace. There, like the hidden treasure in a perfectly cooked omelette, you'll uncover the review button. We would be deeply grateful if you could grace us with your honest rating and a brief, flavorful sentence capturing your egg-sperience.

Every review is a seasoning for us. They're the secret ingredient that makes our cookbook truly crackling, and they mean more than the perfect flip of a well-made omelette. In the spirit of transparency, should you stumble upon a minor hiccup within these pages, please know we've whisked and folded our best efforts into this eggstravaganza. We're not infallible, and, much like a slightly overcooked egg, small mistakes can happen. We hope you can enjoy the overall egg-sperience despite these minor imperfections.

Your support, conveyed through a review, is like the perfect pairing of eggs and toast—it completes the meal and inspires us to keep cracking and cooking delightful creations. So, please, take a moment, and let your words be the extra sprinkle of chives on our egg masterpiece.

We deeply appreciate your time, your discerning palate, and your love for the art of egg cookery. After all, this cookbook isn't just about recipes; it's about celebrating the versatile world of eggs with fellow egg enthusiasts. With sincere gratitude and a toast to perfectly runny yolks, we eagerly await your feedback. May your future egg adventures be as delightful as a perfectly poached egg!